ARE YOU A~~~~~~~~~ ~~ YOUR DOG?

Sure-Fire Wa~~~~~~~~~~~~~~~~~~~~~~~~~mile
As ~~~~~~~~~~~~~~~~~

Alan Cohen
Illustrations by Alan Gordon

ARE YOU AS HAPPY AS YOUR DOG?
Sure-Fire Ways To Wake Up With A Smile
As Big As Your Pooch's

© 1996 by Alan Cohen – ISBN 0-910367-29-9

Alan Cohen Publications
430 Kukuna Road
Haiku, Hawaii 96708
808 572-0001

Illustrations by Alan Gordon
Graphic Design by Carol Sjolander
Cover Design by Daya Ceglia

To Order
ARE YOU AS HAPPY AS YOUR DOG?

Bookstores , Contact:
Bookpeople   DeVorss & Co.   New Leaf
Peaceful Living   Quest

———————

Personal Orders – Call
800-462-3013
or write to:
Hay House, Inc.
Post Office Box 5100
Carlsbad, CA 92018-5100

For a free catalog of Alan Cohen's
Books, tapes, and workshop schedule,
Call or write the above
Address or phone number.

Visit Alan Cohen's website at www.alancohen.com

ALSO BY ALAN COHEN

BOOKS
Dare To Be Yourself
A Deep Breath Of Life
The Dragon Doesn't Live Here Anymore*
Handle With Prayer*
Have You Hugged A Monster Today?
I Had It All The Time*
Joy Is My Compass
Lifestyles Of The Rich In Spirit
The Peace That You Seek
Rising In Love
Setting The Seen

* indicates available as book on audio tape

AUDIO CASSETTES / CD
Deep Relaxation
Eden Morning
I Believe In You
Journey to the Center of the Heart (al CD)
Peace

VIDEO
Dare To Be Yourself
The Wisdom of the Spirit
Alan Cohen: The Inner View

I met a man who told me, "For years I was so miserable that I prayed to God daily to let me wake up as happy as my dog!"

I went home and thought about it. Am I as happy as my dog? Hmmmm.

I began to observe my dog Munchie (short for Munchkin), who is happy all the time. Munchie is the most joyful creature I have ever seen. He lives in a state of continuous delight and discovery.

It became clear to me that Munchie knew something I didn't know (or at least didn't remember). So I decided to study Munchie's attitude to see what he was doing that I was missing.

Here is what I learned from my pet about how to be happy:

As soon as Munchie hears my car pull up to the garage, he drops whatever he is doing and zooms to meet me. He barks and cries at the same time, wags his tail so hard that he wipes up the garage floor with his fuzzy butt, and he tinkles. (Munchie taught me the meaning of the phrase, "I could hardly contain myself!")

Munchie gives me the same whole - hearted greeting no matter how long I have been away. When I come home after a long time he doesn't sit on his haunches with his arms folded and soberly announce, "I think it's time we discussed your commitment to our relationship." He is just happy to see me, and he lets me know it.

LOVE TO BE A LOVER

Munchie is fully present, whatever he is doing. He has no sense of the past or future. You will not find Munchie at a local bar nursing a beer over lost love. He has no lost love. He loves whatever is before him.

BE HERE NOW

Munchie regularly shows up at my front door asking to come in and play with me. Depending on what I am doing and how muddy his feet are, sometimes I let him in. The moment I open the door, he *charges* in. He doesn't give me a moment to change my mind. He knows what he wants, asks for it, and seizes his opportunity the moment it is offered. Munchie is a master of *Carpe Diem.*

SEIZE THE DAY

I never have to figure out what's on Munchie's mind.

When he is happy, he wags his tail. If he isn't feeling well, he cries.

When he wants to play, he jumps into my lap. When he doesn't feel like playing, he walks away.

Munchie has never lied to me, and I trust him.

BE HONEST

When we go to the beach, the only creatures without bathing suits are little children and Munchie. He is not ashamed of his body.

At social gatherings, he goes to sleep on his back with his underbelly and private parts showing.

When Munchie passes doggie gas, he doesn't blame it on invisible animals or "trouser ghosts."

When he sees a cute French Poodle, he gets visibly excited. He accepts his body as natural. Munchie accepts everything as natural.

QUIT HIDING

On cold nights Munchie jumps up into my bed and crawls under the covers.

When he sees me going for a walk he follows me.

When he spies an attractive tree he tugs on his leash.

When I open my car door he tries to jump in.

Munchie knows it's okay to have desires. When he wants something, he makes it plain and clear. Sometimes he gets it and sometimes he doesn't. At least he asked.

ASK FOR WHAT YOU WANT

If you want to learn the power of one-pointed concentration, watch Munchie keep his eye on the tennis ball as I am getting ready to throw it.

I swear, his eye does not leave it for a moment. I can change the hand that holds the ball, put it behind my back, or stuff it in my pocket, and he does not miss a movement.

If I would just stick to my goals as intently as his eye sticks to the ball, I could get everything I ever wanted.

KEEP YOUR EYE ON THE BALL

When Munchie is tired, he sleeps; when he is rested he gets up.

He eats when he is hungry, and walks away from his bowl when his tummy is full.

When someone pets him, he stays right where he is and groans with delight. When he is in pain he stops what he is doing.

When he finds a sunny spot on the grass, he lies down and naps. When the weather is bad he stays in the house.

He moves his body a lot, and he feels good.

LISTEN TO YOUR BODY

Munchie's tail was run over by a car he was chasing. To heal, he laid down on his mat and rested. Whenever I passed his little nook, there was the Munchster, lying quietly with his snout on his paws, allowing nature to do its part.

After a few days he was back in action, barking, tinkling on the garage floor, and charging the house in hopes of getting a biscuit.

I thought about what some of us humans might do if we were injured. We might just keep chasing cars, work harder, or blame someone and waste time complaining. Munchie let all of that go in favor of his natural wisdom. He was smart enough to rest when he needed to, and loved himself enough to do it.

TAKE CARE OF YOURSELF

Munchie has never heard of the Puritan Work Ethic. (His philosophy is closer to the Pure Tan Play Ethic.)

He doesn't punch a clock, get nervous when mortgage interest rates rise, or yell at the television when Rush Limbaugh comes on.

He trusts that life will take care of him, and he doesn't struggle.

Munchie knows that his purpose in life is to enjoy the adventure.

RELAX

When I am not at home Munchie finds plenty of amusements. He chases cats, sniffs dead frogs, naps, and visits neighbors.

The world, through Munchie's eyes, is a big playground. There is always someone or something to keep his life exciting.

Munchie doesn't need an excuse to have fun. Everything is an invitation to play.

He doesn't divide life up into work and play. He finds joy wherever he is.

ENTERTAIN YOURSELF

Sometimes I would swear that Munchie is laughing. His little doggie lips pull back and he pants as if he knows something I don't.

What really annoys me is that he seems to laugh when I have taken myself too seriously.

Maybe he is trying to tell me something.

LAUGH AT YOURSELF

During walks when we get away from the road I let Munchie off his leash. As soon as he feels free, he dashes off into the bushes, where he sniffs to his heart's content and lifts his leg more often than a ballet dancer. He loves to be liberated.

Sure, we have responsibilities, and it's important to take care of them.

But it's also important to cut loose when we can and let our spirit be as free as the wind.

We were born without a leash and we leave this world without a leash. While we're here, we need to give our soul room to breathe.

GET OFF THE LEASH
OCCASIONALLY

When Munchie trusts someone, he is fully present with them.

When he doesn't like someone, he steers clear of them.

He doesn't stay with people who hurt him.

He has no concept that he *has* to be with anyone. He does not suffer to pay off karma from past lives. He does not wrestle with codependency issues.

He is loyal to his friends and lets everyone else go their way.

CHOOSE YOUR RELATIONSHIPS

My dog has no questions about his right to his space. He knows his territory, and he protects it.

The moment any foreign object with wheels or legs comes near the house, his hair-trigger bark alarm goes off. Night or day, he's there to announce potential intruders. (If they don't run away when he approaches, he starts kissing them; we're working on that one.)

Munchie's intention is so strong that he intimidates big dogs. Sometimes a Doberman comes around, and she yields to the Munchie Security Service. The fact that he is no bigger than a rabbit doesn't matter; he knows his rights, and his neighbors honor them.

34

PROTECT YOUR BOUNDARIES

When Munchie meets a dog on the beach, they sniff each other for a while.

Sometimes they make friends and play for a long time, and sometimes they just keep going on their own paths.

I've met a lot of people who, after failed marriages, admitted. "I wish I'd sniffed him a little more before I went home with him."

Sometimes a few extra sniffs now can save a long time living with a really bad smell.

GET TO KNOW SOMEONE
BEFORE YOU COMMIT

When Munchie gets tired during long walks, I pick him up and carry him for a while. The moment he is in my arms, he rolls onto his back and lets me bear him fully.

Harboring no guilt or unworthiness, he does not protest, "You really don't need to do this," or "I will carry you tomorrow." He just lays there and soaks it in.

Munchie knows he is worth the love he receives, and he accepts it.

LET THE LOVE IN

Munchie loves to be a lover. He doesn't withhold love from others, for he knows that he would lose it himself.

You need to love someone as much as you need someone to love you.

People in nursing homes, prisons, and rehabilitation centers become healthy more quickly if they have a pet to take care of.

Care for a person, plant or animal, and sadness will disappear.

Just as it is impossible to whistle and chew crackers at the same time, you cannot give love and be depressed.

GIVE YOUR HEART
TO SOMEONE

Munchie displays his affection eagerly, immediately, and without reserve.

If he likes you he will jump on you and kiss you until you surrender or get up.

My dog loves me, and he lets me know. I like that.

KISS PROFUSELY

Munchie's loyalties are not divided. I'm his person and he's my dog.

We both have lots of friends that fulfill our other interests and needs, but his tag has my phone number on it, and although I do not wear a tag, his number is etched in my heart.

I think about him when I am away, and I make sure he is taken care of if I am not there.

He has never missed a meal, and I have never missed his love.

BE THERE

Munchie doesn't need to impress anyone or prove himself. He is what he is, and that is enough.

He is not concerned about his social image. He is concerned with being happy.

He attracts mud, burrs, and dingleberries.

I can usually tell what he had for breakfast, since it hangs out on his chin for a while.

When I take him to the beach he comes out of the ocean looking like the rat from the vat.

I think he is cute all the time, and he seems to agree.

DARE TO BE YOURSELF

Munchie deals with what is in front of him. He does not schedule into the next decade or wrestle with the decision over whether to lease or buy the car. None of his brain cells are occupied remembering various PIN numbers.

All of life is exactly where he is.

KEEP IT SIMPLE

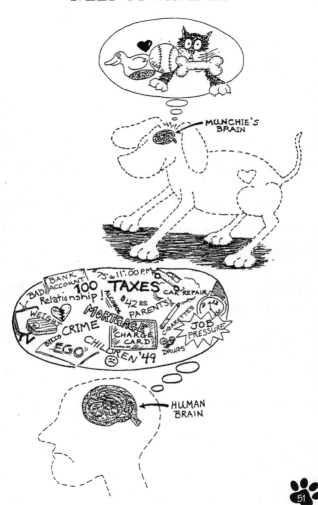

I can say just about anything to Munchie, and he doesn't get upset.

Sometimes after he eats dead frogs he comes home with breath that would make a camel wince.

When I tell him this, he just looks at me and laughs.

He has no ego. Maybe he is better off.

DON'T TAKE IT PERSONALLY

Munchie doesn't hold grudges. When you live in the present moment, what do you have to remember?

Sometimes I accidentally step on his toe. He yelps for a moment and backs away. A few seconds later he is back.

After observing children, psychologists tell us that a healthy amount of time to feel an emotion is five to eight minutes. If it lingers past that, we are holding onto something.

Munchie could have told them that.

GET OVER IT

When the Munchster and I come to a fence that he can't climb, he squeezes under it.

In olden times people had a high value on humility. If you're too puffed up, you can't get through a lot of openings.

If you're willing to be flexible, you can get through lots of spaces that an arrogant dog couldn't.

IF YOU CAN'T GET OVER IT, GO UNDER IT

If I run out of dog food and buy an inferior brand until I can get the good stuff again, Munchie refuses to eat it.

He sits in front of his bowl, looks at his food, and then stares at me as if to say, *"Are you serious?"*

Then he walks away. He knows what he is worth, and doesn't compromise.

DON'T SETTLE FOR MUSH

Munchie has no bank account, makes no mortgage payments, carries no credit cards, doesn't subscribe to Blue Shield, and doesn't fret and scheme at tax time.

Yet he eats well every day, has a lovely little home, gets taken to the vet when he needs it, enjoys plenty of friends who love him, and has everything he needs to be happy.

He must know something I forgot.

TRUST THE FORCE

If something in the outer world can make you high, its absence can make you low.

Munchie doesn't depend on a sub-stance or a particular person to make him feel good.

He just decides to feel good, and his world revolves around his original choice.

THE BEST BISCUITS ARE INSIDE

No one ever told Munchie that he was little, so he acts big.

When I take him on walks through the country, he chases cows and horses. I think they are more surprised than intimidated to be corralled by a barking tumbleweed. But it works. Munch usually gets the critters to move at least a little bit, and he comes back with a triumphant smile.

Once he got a cement truck to stop. He sat in front of it and barked until it came to a halt.

Munchie thinks big, and so he lives big.

THINK BIG

Munchie assumes that his motivations are worthwhile. He lives as if he belongs here.

He doesn't dissect every thought and action, wondering if his desire for a bone springs from a deep unresolved Oedipal fixation.

Munchie does not lie awake at night wondering if he exists. He is here, and that is proof enough.

He knows that "DOG" is "GOD" spelled backwards.

He is enlightened, because he has never been endarkened.

BELIEVE IN YOURSELF

Every few months Munchie disappears for several days. Once I went searching for him and found him at a house down the road, trying to romance a German shepherd. The little guy reached no higher than the big lady's knee, but that didn't stop him.

At least he tried.

THINK POSSIBILITY

Pick a goal that is beyond your limits, then sing to it.

You may get it.

Even if you don't, you'll have fun singing.

HOWL AT THE MOON

When Munchie dreams, his little feet move as if he is running. I imagine he is dreaming of chasing cats, and he is so excited that his legs have to do something even though he's asleep.

If you want to make your dreams come true, do something about them, even while you are dreaming.

Don't wait until you are done dreaming, 'cause then it might be too late.

DREAM
WITH YOUR FEET MOVING

When we go for walks Munchie loves to poke his nose in holes, run into unfamiliar fields, and meet new people.

He is not satisfied with the familiar.

Sometimes he gets his nose stung, but most of the time his world keeps expanding.

VENTURE INTO NEW TERRITORY

When Munchie and I go hiking over rocks up a stream, sometimes we come to boulders that are hundreds of times his size.

Does this stop the Munchster? Of course not!

Munchie steps back, scans the terrain, and takes a different route over a number of smaller rocks. By the time I am on top of the big rock, so is he.

He found the way that worked for him, and did whatever he needed to get where he wanted to go.

WHATEVER IT TAKES

Munchie is one persistent little fella.

If he wants a dog biscuit, he will sit at the foot of the dining room table and look sad, hungry - even starving - until you supply him.

His will usually outlasts mine.

Don't quit now; one more try, and you might have it.

HANG IN THERE

When Munchie digs in the sand at the beach, he doesn't stop until he hits bedrock.

Sometimes he finds a treasure, and sometimes he doesn't. But he never stops until he has moved every bit of sand out of his way.

While he is digging, you could not distract him with all the Milkbones in the world.

When he is done, he walks away, triumphant. He went all the way.

GO ALL THE WAY

No matter where he wanders and how long he is gone, Munchie comes home.

He has a place in the world that is his. His body fits onto his pillow, his bowl has his name on it, and his little house has his very own smell.

Everybody needs a pillow, bowl, and smell they can call their own.

COME HOME

As far as I can tell, Munchie is an enlightened being. He doesn't read a lot of books, has never gone to a seminar, and has no problem balancing his checkbook. Perhaps, if I play my cards right, one day I will wake up as happy as him.

ALAN COHEN

Alan Cohen's books and seminars have touched the hearts and changed the lives of hundreds of thousands of people seeking more aliveness, authenticity, and creative self-expression. He resides in Maui, Hawaii, where he conducts inspirational retreats and plays with Munchie.

ALAN GORDON

Alan Gordon is a free lance artist, cartoonist and real estate broker, living with his wife, Gilda, in Blowing Rock, North Carolina.

For more information
about Alan Gordon's art
contact him at
PO Box 2635
Blowing Rock, NC 28605